GALE

CENGAGE Learning

# Drama for Students, Volume 13

*Staff*

**Editor:** Elizabeth Thomason.

**Contributing Editors:** Reginald Carlton, Anne Marie Hacht, Michael L. LaBlanc, Ira Mark Milne, Jennifer Smith.

**Managing Editor, Content:** Dwayne D. Hayes.

**Managing Editor, Product:** David Galens.

**Publisher, Literature Product:** Mark Scott.

**Literature Content Capture:** Joyce Nakamura, *Managing Editor.* Michelle Poole, *Associate Editor.*

**Research:** Victoria B. Cariappa, *Research Manager.* Cheryl Warnock, *Research Specialist.* Tamara Nott, Tracie A. Richardson, *Research Associates.* Nicodemus Ford, Sarah Genik, Timothy Lehnerer, Ron Morelli, *Research Assistants.*

**Permissions:** Maria Franklin, *Permissions*

*Manager*. Debra J. Freitas, Jacqueline Jones, Julie Juengling, *Permissions Assistants*.

**Manufacturing:** Mary Beth Trimper, *Manager, Composition and Electronic Prepress*. Evi Seoud, *Assistant Manager, Composition Purchasing and Electronic Prepress*. Stacy Melson, *Buyer*.

**Imaging and Multimedia Content Team:** Barbara Yarrow, *Manager*. Randy Bassett, *Imaging Supervisor*. Robert Duncan, Dan Newell, *Imaging Specialists*. Pamela A. Reed, *Imaging Coordinator*. Leitha Etheridge-Sims, Mary Grimes, David G. Oblender, *Image Catalogers*. Robyn V. Young, *Project Manager*. Dean Dauphinais, *Senior Image Editor*. Kelly A. Quin, *Image Editor*.

**Product Design Team:** Kenn Zorn, *Product Design Manager*. Pamela A. E. Galbreath, *Senior Art Director*. Michael Logusz, *Graphic Artist*.

individual does not imply endorsement of the editors or publisher. Errors brought to the attention of the publisher and verified to the satisfaction of the publisher will be corrected in future editions.

©2001 Gale Group
27500 Drake Rd.
Farmington Hills, MI 48331-3535

Gale Group and Design is a trademark used herein under license.

This book is printed on acid-free paper that meets the minimum requirements of American National Standard for Information Sciences—Permanence Paper for Printed Library Materials, ANSIZ39.48-1984.

ISBN 0-7876-4087-5
ISSN 1094-9232

Printed in the United States of America
10 9 8 7 6 5 4 3 2 1

# Seascape

Edward Albee 1975

## Introduction

With *Seascape,* American playwright Edward Albee won his second Pulitzer Prize for drama. Albee himself directed this Broadway production, which opened on January 26, 1975, at the Sam S. Shubert Theatre. The play was published by Atheneum that same year. Like many of Albee's plays, *Seascape* focuses on communication in interpersonal relationships, in this case between couples. Albee's first successful play, *Who's Afraid of Virginia Woolf?* (1962), and his first Pulitzer Prize-winning play, A *Delicate Balance* (1966), also concerned this topic. *Seascape* is different from these dramas on several counts. The play is not strictly a drama but, according to various critics, has elements of comedy, fantasy, satire, and/or absurdism. In *Seascape,* Nancy and Charlie, an American couple on the verge of the major life change of retirement, are having problems in their relationship. They are discussing these matters on the beach when another couple appears, two human-sized lizards named Leslie and Sarah who speak and act like people. The lizards have evolved to such a degree that they no longer feel at home in the sea and are compelled to seek life on the land. What the lizards experience with Nancy and Charlie nearly drives them back to the sea, but with an offer of help from the human couple, they decide to stay. This relatively happy ending is not common in many of Albee's previous plays, and some critics find it refreshing. Critics are divided in their opinion of the play and its content. Some believe it is witty and original, while others find it to be pompous if not gimmicky, primarily because of the lizard characters. One critic who found *Seascape* noteworthy, Clive Barnes of the *New York Times,* writes, "it is a curiously compelling exploration into the basic tenet of life. It is asking in a lighthearted but heavy-minded fashion whether life is worth living. It decides that there is no alternative."

# Author Biography

Edward Franklin Albee was born March 12, 1928, probably in the state of Virginia. His place of birth is unknown because Albee was adopted when he was two weeks old in Washington, D.C., by a wealthy couple, Reed A. Albee and his third wife Frances. Reed A. Albee was the son of Edward Albee, Jr., a founder of the Keith-Albee theater circuit. The year Albee was born, Reed Albee retired from his work as part owner of the Keith-Albee. Albee grew up in a household filled with people from the theater and regularly attended theatrical events from an early age.

Albee's childhood was also unconventional in other ways. He had a privileged life, but his parents' marriage was strained, in part because of his domineering mother. Their problems proved a source of inspiration for Albee's plays. Because his father was retired, the family traveled regularly during the school year, interrupting Albee's early education. By the time Albee was eleven, he had been enrolled in and kicked out of several boarding schools. He finally graduated from the Choate School in 1949. After graduation, Albee spent three semesters studying at Trinity College.

Having become estranged from his parents when he was eighteen—in part because Albee admitted his homosexuality—he survived in New York City's Greenwich Village on a trust fund set up by his beloved maternal grandmother and by holding odd jobs, including delivering messages for Western Union. For the next ten years, Albee absorbed New York City's cultural life and concentrated on his own writing. He primarily wrote poetry, but he also wrote novels and short stories. The theater still intrigued him, but he only turned out one or two plays (none of them produced) before he turned thirty.

On his thirtieth birthday, Albee quit his job and began writing a play. This was *Zoo Story,* which was first produced in West Berlin, Germany, in 1959, after being rejected by New York producers. The following year, it was produced in New York to some acclaim, and it won several prestigious awards. Albee began to make his name as a young playwright first with short plays, then with his first massive success, *Who's Afraid of Virginia Woolf?* (1962). This full-length drama is about a quarreling couple. Albee had mixed success with most of his subsequent plays in the 1960s. His only true success was another play about a troubled relationship, *A Delicate Balance* (1966), which won Albee his first Pulitzer Prize.

Albee produced only a few plays of note in the 1970s through the early 1990s. Only *Seascape* (1975), which won Albee his second Pulitzer Prize, attracted any positive critical attention. Though many of his original and adapted plays were produced, most met with little or no success, especially in New York City. They were often produced abroad and in regional theaters. Albee's most recent important play was 1991 's *Three Tall Women,* which was inspired by Albee's mother. When the play made its way to New York City in 1994, it received positive reviews and Albee's third Pulitzer Prize. Albee continues to write plays in the twenty-first century and also teaches playwriting at the University of Houston.

## *Act1*

*Seascape* opens on a beach. An older couple, Nancy and Charlie, has finished a picnic lunch. As Nancy cleans up, the noise of a jet flying low engulfs the stage. Charlie predicts that a jet will someday smash into a dune.

Nancy expresses her desire to be near the water forever. She loves everything about it and would like to travel from beach to beach. Charlie responds negatively to her dreams. He does not want to do anything or go anywhere.

Charlie's attitude angers Nancy. She points out that life is short. She threatens to have adventures on her own. Charlie's attitude changes after Nancy's outburst, and she retreats from her plan a bit. She is content to enjoy the moment.

After another jet passes by, Nancy reminds Charlie about his childhood desire to live under the water. Charlie tells her how he would sink to the bottom of a pool or lake and sit there until he had to breathe. Nancy encourages him to do this again and get in touch with his youth. Charlie refuses, embarrassed by her insistence.

Nancy changes the subject to their sex life. She tells him about a time in their marriage when she thought of divorcing him. There was tension, and she suspected that he was having an affair. Charlie denies this, and Nancy accepts his word.

Nancy encourages him to sink under the water again and to show her how he did it. Charlie again refuses and turns the conversation to her. He tells her that she was a good wife. Nancy says the same about him, listing the many ways in which he was a good husband. When she is done, she is bitter because the "good life" they have had seems limited to her. Charlie is hurt by her attitude. They argue. Nancy is still angry that his only interest is to rest, while she wants to experience new things.

During a pause at the end of their heated argument, Leslie, a human-sized male lizard, takes a peek at them. Nancy tries to get Charlie to help write postcards, but he declines. Leslie peeks at them again, this time with his female mate, Sarah. Nancy sees the lizards and is intrigued. Charlie is afraid.

Charlie demands that Nancy find him something to defend them with. When she can only find a small, thin stick, Charlie is peeved. Nancy remains interested in the lizards, but when Leslie clears his throat, she fears the lizards might hurt them.

When Leslie waves his large stick, Nancy and Charlie admit their love for each other, Nancy more reluctantly than Charlie. As Leslie and Sarah move forward, another jet flies by and scares them away. Charlie tries to blame the whole episode on bad liver paste sandwiches. He believes they are dead from food poisoning. Nancy ridicules the idea.

Nancy is pleased when Leslie and Sarah return. To protect themselves, Nancy believes they should show submission by lying on their back with their legs and arms up, as a dog would. Charlie assumes the position, though with great reluctance.

## *Act 2*

Act 2 opens where act 1 ended. Leslie and Sarah are unsure about Nancy and Charlie's submissive stance. When Leslie and Sarah approach, Charlie threatens to scream. Nancy is much calmer. Leslie pokes Charlie and Nancy in the side, but neither one moves. Leslie and Sarah decide that Nancy and Charlie are relatively harmless.

Charlie is unsure about the creatures, while Nancy is fascinated by everything about them. Leslie and Sarah decide to approach them again. Leslie pokes Charlie hard, causing Charlie to speak. Leslie replies several times, but Charlie will not speak to the creature. Nancy finally sits up and greets Sarah. Charlie only says hello after Nancy encourages him.

Sarah and Nancy believe that the tension has been diffused, but Leslie and Charlie are still uncertain of each other. With Nancy's prodding, Charlie assures Leslie that they are not unfriendly. Though Leslie and Sarah speak English, they do not understand many of the words and ideas that Charlie and Nancy use.

Nancy tries to shake Leslie's flipper, but Leslie cannot grasp the concept. Nancy and Charlie explain the concept of the handshake, as well as their differing anatomy. The lizards have only legs and flippers. Nancy finally shakes hands with the lizards. Charlie tries to shake hands with Leslie, but Leslie is still uncertain about him. Leslie and Charlie talk about their differences. Leslie asks about their clothing. Among other things, Nancy tells them that clothes cover their sexual organs.

This leads to a discussion of the humans' sex organs, especially Nancy's breasts. The lizards do not have these organs. Nancy shows Sarah, who is fascinated. Leslie also wants to see, but Charlie is uncomfortable with the idea. To change the subject, Charlie asks about their children. Sarah and Leslie have produced seven thousand eggs. Leslie is appalled when he learns that the humans do not lay eggs. Nancy explains human gestation and that they have three children.

When Nancy tells them that they keep their children for many years, she also explains the concept of love. This and all other emotions are foreign concepts to the lizards. Charlie asks how Sarah and Leslie became paired. Leslie fought off other lizards when Sarah reached her maturity and started to mate. He wanted her, but emotions did not play a role.

Charlie brings up the idea of disloyalty in Leslie and Sarah's relationship. This upsets Nancy. The issue also confuses Sarah and Leslie. Charlie is nearly attacked by Leslie when he angrily compares the male lizard to a fish. The women calm the men down and Leslie explains his disdainful attitude toward fish. They discuss the ideas of prejudice and difference.

Sarah looks up and sees birds flying by. Leslie becomes defensive. Nancy explains to Sarah that the birds are seagulls. The females compare them to underwater rays. Nancy tells Sarah that she has seen photographs of rays. Nancy and Charlie cannot explain what photography is to her, so Sarah believes they are insulting her. When Leslie returns, Sarah explains what has happened.

Abruptly changing the subject, Nancy declares that Charlie believes that they are dead. She continues to dig into Charlie, sarcastically saying that no wonders are possible. Leslie and Sarah catch on to her meaning, to some degree, but Leslie is confused by the idea that reality is an illusion. When Leslie asks Charlie to explain it, Charlie becomes angry.

After Nancy calms him down, another jet flies by. Leslie and Sarah are fearful. Nancy and Charlie explain the idea of the airplane. Charlie talks about other machines including those that go undersea. Nancy tells the lizards about the times in Charlie's youth when he would sink under water and stay there. Angry at Nancy, Charlie changes the subject and asks the lizards why they came out of the sea in the first place. They do not know, other than they have changed somehow and do not belong there anymore.

This prompts Charlie to explain the idea of evolution, but Leslie and Sarah do not understand it fully. The lizards can only think in terms of themselves. When Sarah asks if progress is good, Charlie is uncertain. Every term and idea has to be explained to the lizards, leading to more frustration for Charlie, as well as Leslie and Sarah.

Charlie asks Sarah what she would do if Leslie went away and did not come back. Nancy becomes angry at him for asking. Sarah is upset by the question and wants to go back to the sea. Leslie hits and chokes Charlie for making Sarah cry. Leslie and Sarah decide to go back. Nancy tells them to stay because eventually they will have to come back. Nancy, and to some degree Charlie, offer their help. Leslie accepts their offer.

# Characters

## *Charlie*

Charlie is married to Nancy and is part of the human couple at the center of the play. Unlike his wife, Charlie is fearful and passive. While Nancy wants to have an active retirement, Charlie wants to rest and do nothing. He does not understand his wife's need to connect with the past and explore the world they have not seen. Charlie admits to having a more adventurous spirit in his youth. He would release his breath and sink to the bottom of pools or other bodies of water until he had to rise to breath again. Charlie liked to do this then but has no desire to do it now. He is content with the way things currently are in his life and does not like to be challenged.

It is Nancy who first antagonizes him. Nancy's idea about living at different beaches for the rest of their lives is distasteful to him. He will not let her push him into even considering such a lifestyle. Nancy later tells him, much to his surprise, that she considered divorcing him a long time ago because she believed he was having an affair. Charlie tells her he did not have such a liaison, and she believes him. Charlie was happy with the way his life with Nancy was and still is. Their disagreements over this matter are overshadowed by the appearance of the lizards.

If Charlie is uncomfortable with Nancy and her desires, he has bigger problems with the lizards. At first, he insists that they are a death hallucination caused by rotten liver paste sandwiches. While the creatures intrigue Nancy, Charlie continually acts with fear and resistance. He follows his wife's lead on posing submissively when the creatures first approach, but he will not respond to them until she orders him to. Even after the ice has been broken, Charlie remains uncertain about the creatures and their intentions. Leslie and Sarah's ignorance on many things (emotions, anatomy, etc.) adds to Charlie's negative attitude. When he has to explain these ideas to them, he is easily frustrated and often condescending. He drives Leslie to beat and choke him. Yet at the end, Charlie agrees with Nancy that the lizards have to stay on land and not go back into the water. Though he helps because Nancy will do it whether or not he agrees, Charlie does offer to take them by the hand.

## Leslie

Leslie is the male lizard who appears at the end of act 1. Like Charlie, Leslie is a bit more fearful, defensive, and mistrusting than his mate. It is he who first watches the human couple. Leslie is also the first to approach Nancy and Charlie, poking them in the side. When Charlie does not reply right away, Leslie becomes frustrated. While Leslie's guard remains high, especially around Charlie, for most of the play, he is also curious, much more so than his human male counterpart.

Both Leslie and Sarah speak English, though they do not understand many words and concepts of human life. Leslie does not know what emotions are, what cooking or clothing is, or what the names of limbs are. When Nancy tries to shake hands with him, he is completely unfamiliar with and mistrustful of the process. Though Leslie wants to understand for the most part, he becomes impatient when the humans cannot easily explain complex things like love or consciousness.

Though Leslie does not possess or understand some human ideas like love, he does have prejudices against others. Charlie tries and fails to explain what bigotry is to the lizard after Leslie speaks badly of fish. Leslie thinks they are dirty and too numerous. He also looks down on humans because they do not lay eggs. Yet Leslie also has some empathy for the humans. Leslie knows that he and Sarah must look odd to Charlie and Nancy. He also understands that Charlie is being difficult when Nancy mentions that her husband thinks they are dead and that this situation is some sort of hallucination.

Leslie acts most often on instinct, like an animal. When birds and jets fly overhead, he runs to find an escape route. Leslie is very protective of Sarah. When Charlie hurts Sarah—asking her what she would do if Leslie left and never came back—Leslie attacks him. After hitting him, Leslie nearly chokes him until the females intercede. After the incident, Leslie decides that he and Sarah will go back into the sea, to escape this threat. When Nancy tells him that they will have to come back eventually and offers them help, it is Leslie who accepts this fate.

## *Nancy*

Nancy is the female half of the human couple in the play; she is married to Charlie. Unlike her husband, Nancy is vibrant and curious about the world. When the play opens, she wants to live at the beach forever. Now that her children are grown, Nancy wants to have adventures. Charlie does not share her desires and does his best to discourage them. Despite Charlie's negative attitude, Nancy remains open to what comes her way, including the lizards.

Nancy's relationship with Charlie is somewhat strained. Nancy is angry at Charlie's passivity. Her attempts to encourage Charlie to sink underwater as he did as a child meet with a negative response. This frustrates her. Over the course of the first act, it is revealed that she once considered divorcing him because she believed that he was having an affair. Though she readily accepts his word when he says he did not, she does not think the "good life" they had together has been all that it could be. Still, Nancy remains loyal to Charlie. While she threatens to have adventures on her own, she does nothing about it.

When the lizards approach them, Nancy is fascinated but a little afraid. She remains close to Charlie. Though she does not agree with him, she does find him a small stick to use as a defense. It is Nancy who comes up with the idea of lying down in a submissive posture when Leslie and Sarah come near. Charlie follows Nancy's directions in most of the dealings with the lizards. After it becomes clear that the lizards will not harm them, Nancy is excited by their presence. She does everything she can to learn about them and make a connection with them. She wants to shake hands with them first.

Charlie is uncomfortable with the lengths to which his wife goes to connect with the lizards. Because Sarah has never seen a mammal's mammaries, Nancy shows Sarah her breasts and explains their function. Nancy would also have shown Leslie except for Charlie's protestations. While Nancy does become a bit frustrated with the lizards' intellectual limitations, she becomes increasingly annoyed with Charlie's condescending attitude toward them. Yet, when the lizards want to go back—after Charlie drives Sarah to tears, and Leslie beats him up—Nancy wants them to stay and offers them help. This experience has given Nancy the excitement she craves, and she ensures that it continues.

## Sarah

Sarah is the female half of the lizard couple, the mate of Leslie. Like her mate, Sarah is cautious and fearful around the humans. Yet like Nancy, she is curious about them and tries to make a connection. Though Sarah defers to Leslie much more than Nancy does to Charlie, she does play a buffer role between the couples. Leslie often consults Sarah on what he should do and what she thinks about the humans and the situation at hand. At first, Sarah urges wariness, but she also emphasizes the importance of contact.

Though Sarah is more deferential than Nancy, she does assert herself to Leslie when an experience is important. For example, she insists on accompanying Leslie when he approaches the humans in act 2 after they have taken their submissive pose. Sarah wants to see everything for herself. Most of the new things she encounters intrigue her: the handshakes; Nancy's breasts; human gestation; and the birds flying above them, among other things. But she is also fearful. The jets frighten her, as does Charlie when he asks her what she would do if Leslie went away and never came back. Like Leslie, Sarah does not grasp many human concepts like emotions and non-aquatic animals, though she tries.

Sarah is also more open to explaining their way of life to the humans than her husband is. Leslie tries to curb her, but Sarah says what she believes she should say. Sarah does not fully share Leslie's prejudices and tries to make the humans understand her. For example, Sarah shares information on their reproduction and how she and Leslie met. It is also Sarah who tells the humans why they decided to come out of the sea. Leslie is reluctant to part with this information.

After Charlie asks the question, which makes

her cry, Sarah wants to go back into the sea. Leslie agrees with her. Later, Sarah intercedes when Leslie tries to beat up Charlie over it. Though Sarah wants to return to their home, Leslie decides, with Nancy's help, to stay.

# Topics for Further Study

- Research the theory of evolution, focusing on the time when scientists theorize that creatures emerged from the water to the land. Using your research, discuss what scientists believed compelled these animals to leave the water and compare this motivation to the depiction of the lizards, Leslie and Sarah, in *Seascape*.

- Explore readings about interpersonal communication and marriage. How could Nancy and Charlie have solved their differences more constructively? Compare their communication style to that of Sarah and Leslie.

- Research the effects of retirement on the retiree and his or her partner. What changes take place? Discuss options Nancy and Charlie could explore as retirees. How does Nancy's dream of moving from beach to beach fit in with your findings?

- Compare and contrast the two couples in *Seascape* with the troubled couple depicted in Albee's famous play, *Who's Afraid of Virginia Woolf?* (1962). What common communication issues do these couples share?

# Themes

## *Communication and Understanding*

At the thematic center of *Seascape* are issues related to communication and understanding. Though all of the characters speak English, when each of the four tries to communicate with the others, only varied success is achieved. The theme of communication takes on several forms in the play.

First, there is the communication between each member of a couple with their respective mate. Nancy tries to engage her husband, Charlie, in a mutually beneficial discussion about her needs and their future, but he derides her ideas. Nancy wants to explore and be adventurous in their retirement, while Charlie wants to rest and do nothing. Throughout the play, their inability to communicate and understand each other's wants and needs creates tension and hostility.

Leslie and Sarah have fewer problems communicating. Leslie is dominant in their relationship, and Sarah is generally content to play a subservient role. Leslie consults Sarah on most decisions and generally respects her input. Sarah speaks up when she feels Leslie is acting inappropriately, and Leslie usually listens.

The other significant form of communication is between the two couples and is different between the genders. Nancy is very curious about and open with the lizards. Though she does become slightly frustrated by their limitations, she tries to help them by explaining aspects of human life they do not understand. Her general kindness toward them and offer of help when the lizards are deciding whether to stay on land or to go back to the sea influences their decision. Charlie is less forthcoming and more suspicious. He has a hard time accepting the lizards and quickly becomes testy when they do not understand his explanations.

The lizards' communication is somewhat similar to their human counterparts. Like Nancy, Sarah is more open to the humans and more interested in their world. She is also emotional, and when Charlie asks her a question that is hard for her to understand (what she would do if Leslie disappeared), she becomes distraught, leading to a confrontation. Leslie shares Charlie's attitude; he does not trust the humans and regards most everything they say with skepticism. Despite these problems, at the end of the play, some measure of trust is reached between all of them. Leslie decides that he and Sarah will stay on land when Nancy and Charlie, albeit reluctantly, offer to help them.

## *Evolution and Progress*

Another prominent theme in *Seascape* is that of evolution and progress. This theme manifests itself in several ways in the play. One is subtle. The relationship of Nancy and Charlie is in the process of evolution. They are on the verge of a major life change, retirement. Charlie would like to use this time to rest and do nothing. Nancy sees this desire as regression rather than evolution. Her family responsibilities fulfilled, Nancy wants to explore the world, perhaps moving from beach to beach, meeting new people, and having new experiences. The couple's relationship will change, and Nancy tries to move it forward. Charlie wants things to stay the same.

Evolution has a different meaning in terms of the lizards. Leslie and Sarah are literally evolving. They were creatures that lived in the sea but apparently developed beyond their species. They were compelled to move to the land, though they do not really understand why. Though Leslie and Sarah are somewhat fearful of the change, they do accept the help that Nancy, enthusiastically, and Charlie, reluctantly, give them. At the end of the play, rather than go back into the sea where they might feel safer, they remain on land.

## *Alienation*

A more subtle undercurrent in *Seascape* is the idea of alienation. In terms of this play, to be alienated means to feel withdrawn or exist in an unfriendly environment. Alienation was one of the reasons that Leslie and Sarah left the sea. In act 2, Sarah tells the humans, "it wasn't. . . comfortable any more. I mean after all, you make your nest, and accept a whole. . . array. .. of things... and... we didn't feel we *belonged* there anymore." It could be argued that this alienation was a step in their evolution. Nancy and, to some degree, Charlie also feel alienated in their lives. In act 1, Nancy describes several ways in which she feels alienated, mostly in her relationship with Charlie. She does not share his views on what their life was, is, and could be; she wants to do more than retire. Though not as vocal, Charlie, in turn, feels alienated from her because of her curiosity and her desires. The strains caused by alienation affect the direction of the characters and the action of the play.

## Setting

*Seascape* is set on a beach in a time contemporary with when the play was written. Though it is unstated in the text, several critics have assumed that the action takes place somewhere on the east coast of the United States. All of the play is confined to one afternoon. This physical setting emphasizes the transitional state of the characters lives. It is one of many symbols in the play.

## Fantasy

There is critical debate over exactly what genre of play *Seascape* is. Some believe it is a comedy, while others see it as absurdist, satirical, or allegorical. Most agree that there is an element of fantasy involved. While Nancy and Charlie are humans and act accordingly, Leslie and Sarah are fantastic creations. They are human-sized lizards that have left their life in the sea to live on land. They speak perfect English and understand some aspects of human life. Charlie has a hard time accepting that they are real. He wants to believe that he and Nancy see them because they are suffering from food poisoning or are dead. In terms of the play, however, Leslie and Sarah are very real, a fact that Nancy immediately grasps and embraces. The fantasy aspect of the play creates dramatic tension and allows issues such as progress, values, and differences to be discussed.

## *Symbolism*

Many symbols are employed by Albee to underscore the action and themes of *Seascape*. The most obvious symbols are the lizard characters, Leslie and Sarah. Because these are anthropomorphic creatures (that is, animals with human qualities), they can be used to illustrate Albee's ideas about humans and their relationships. Leslie and Sarah represent many things, including a literal depiction of evolution and progress and an ideal of a relationship that works in stark contrast to Nancy and Charlie's relationship.

The setting itself is also symbolic. The beach —where land and sea meet—represents a place of progress. In the theory of evolution, creatures emerged from the sea to live on land like Leslie and Sarah do in the course of the play. Changes for all four characters are taking place at the beach. Another symbol is the jet planes that zoom overhead. The jets are another symbol of progress, but a more mixed one than those already discussed. The jets are described to Sarah as the mechanical evolution of the seagulls that fascinate her. Yet Charlie worries that a jet will one day crash into the dune—a temporary if not symbolic end to evolution. The jets also scare both Sarah and Leslie. But the jets continue to fly and never crash, and the lizards decide to embrace their evolution. Though

feared by everyone but Nancy in *Seascape,* change
seems endorsed by the play's complex symbolism.

## *Family Life*

In the 1970s, American society was in transition, undergoing radical changes in a number of areas including family life. The 1970s were known as the "me" decade; people were passive and self-absorbed, concerned primarily with their own personal happiness and self-fulfillment. During this era, the divorce rate rose, and there were more nontraditional families because of divorce and remarriage. Another prominent aspect of this time period was the "empty nest syndrome." Children who left home at the age of eighteen to attend college did not return after graduation. Because there were no children in the home, many mothers felt loss. Women's lives changed. Some entered the workforce or continued their own education; others did volunteer work.

## *Women and Feminism*

As women's role in the home changed, so did their role in society. Some historians consider the burgeoning feminist movement of the 1970s as one of the most important social elements of the decade. The women's movement emerged from the social revolution of the 1960s and shared many aspects with the civil rights movement. Through the efforts of feminists, the Equal Rights Amendment (ERA) was passed by the senate in 1972 and was ratified by states throughout the decade. Similar to the Civil Rights Acts, this amendment to the Constitution would have guaranteed equal rights for women under the law in a number of areas. The ERA was never ratified by three-quarters of the states as required by law and thus it ultimately failed. Its failure was due in part to the efforts of those who feared change in society. Some believed empowering women would destroy the family.

Though the ERA failed, women's issues were addressed by legislation that was passed by federal and state legislatures as well as court rulings. Because more women were entering the workforce (about forty percent of the workforce was women in 1975), sex discrimination was outlawed in a number of areas, including the right to have pensions and nondiscrimination in hiring. More educational opportunities were opened to women. In 1972, Title IX of the Educational Amendments Act guaranteed women equal access to higher education and athletic opportunities. Despite such positive steps, many women did not receive equal pay for equal work. Women sometimes earned only two-thirds to three-quarters of what men earned for performing the same job.

The year 1975 was particularly important to women on a global scale. It was declared the International Women's Year by the United Nations.

## Compare & Contrast

- **1975:** Though it is the International Women's Year, many women in the workplace face discrimination, especially in terms of pay. Women generally earn about a quarter to a third less than men for doing the same work as men.

  **Today:** Though the "glass ceiling" has been broken and many more women work, women still generally earn only about 80 to 90 percent of the salary of their male counterparts.

- **1975:** Organic foods are a relatively new concept, a fad among hippies concerned with environmental and ecological issues. Their availability is limited but growing.

  **Today:** Organic farming is an accepted practice, and organic foods can be found in many grocery stores.

- **1975:** There is controversy over the effects of the use of aerosol cans on the environment, especially the ozone layer. Within a few years, their use is regulated.

  **Today:** The hole in the ozone layer has grown significantly since the 1970s. Though the use of aerosol cans is regulated, many scientists agree that their use played a role in the hole's size.

- **1975:** The United States is still recovering from the OPEC crisis of 1973-1974. The crisis limited the amount of oil that the United States could import, creating an energy crisis. Many called for the exploration of alternative sources of energy.

  **Today:** The use of alternative energy in the United States remains limited, though the calls for its exploration are ongoing. American consumption of oil has not decreased, and some have considered drilling untouched, hard-to-reach places under the sea to find more oil.

---

Among the events was a conference sponsored by the United Nations in Mexico City, Mexico. Women representing countries around the world gathered to talk about women's issues and to work to improve their status.

## *Environmental Issues*

In the 1970s, environmental and ecological concerns took center stage in the United States. Many people spoke out about the impact of industry on the environment. There was widespread interest in environmental organizations like the Sierra Club.

Of particular concern were air and water quality, and the limiting of pollution. The Environmental Protection Agency (EPA) encouraged water conservation by regulating the quality of drinking water. Environmental laws affected the licensing of nuclear power plants. One controversy of the time period focused on the regulation of the height of smokestacks: the taller they were the more pollution they could emit because it could be spread over a wider area making it seem as if the actual amount of pollution was less. Other concerns included the disposal of radioactive waste and the affects of aerosol cans on the ozone layer. Within a few years, these cans came under strict scrutiny.

Dissatisfaction with urban life and related problems led to a back to earth/New Age movement, primarily among hippies. A significant number of hippies moved from cities to rural communities to farm organic food. Because of concerns with farming practices, including the potential danger of pesticides, growth regulators, and other synthetic compounds, organic food became a fad during this era. Organic food was grown using "natural" biological practices. This fad soon became a common and accepted method of farming.

# Critical Overview

Before Albee won the Pulitzer Prize for drama for *Seascape,* many critics reacted negatively to the first production. Only a few had generally positive responses. One was Clive Barnes of the *New York Times* who writes, "What Mr. Albee has given us here is a play of great density, with many interesting emotional and intellectual reverberations." *The Nation's* Harold Clurman places *Seascape* in a positive context in terms of Albee's development as a playwright. He believes, "It is his most relaxed play, a 'philosophical' whimsy. You may find it delightful. ... It is a step in Albee's still green career, a step which, seen in a certain light, augurs well for the future. In an agreeable sense, it is a 'little' play."

Other critics had a more mixed response to *Seascape.*While they found something to praise, other aspects brought the experience down for them. John Beaufort of the *Christian Science Monitor* writes, "As cerebral comedies go, *Seascape* is provocative and tantalizing rather than profound, and perhaps too whimsical for its own good." Edwin Wilson of the *Wall Street Journal* wants more from Albee. He argues, "The disappointing thing is that the playwright, having given himself a theatrical device with potential and the performers to make it work, has proceeded to squander his opportunities."

Many critics who wrote mixed reviews

commented on Albee's use of language. This had been a positive point in many of Albee's previous plays and critics were divided over its success in *Seascape*.Howard Kissel of *Women's Wear Daily* believes, "Albee's lines have a pleasurable cadence, a naturally engaging rhythm even if they seldom grow out of character or intensify the admittedly diffuse drama." In his more negative review, Jack Kroll of *Newsweek* writes, "in *Seascape* that long-windedness has become a constipated language that moves in colonic spasms. . . . Albee achieves only the ultimate in pure nagging."

A number of critics could find little redeeming value to *Seascape*.Commenting on the use of the lizards, Stanley Kauffmann of the *New Republic* writes,"This is hardly a startlingly original idea for a play, but it's not a bad one. The play itself *is* bad— because it is nothing more than its idea." The *New York Post's* Martin Gottfried shares Kauffmann's negative opinion. Gottfried argues, "There is no way for *Seascape* to be touching because there is so little craftsmanship in it, so little artistry and, crucially, so little humanity and heart."

After its original run and its Pulitzer Prize, *Seascape* was still performed on a regular basis, primarily in repertory productions. Critical opinion generally became more positive with time. Of a 1996 production in San Francisco, Steven Winn of the *San Francisco Chronicle* writes, "Fanciful and philosophical, like many of the playwright's more abstruse chamber pieces, it also flashes the combustive marital combat and dismay that ignited

*Who's Afraid of Virginia Woolf?* 34 years ago." However, not all critics were completely positive. Of a 1998 production in Los Angeles, Robert Koehler of the *Los Angeles Times* argues, "Even when Edward Albee is not at his best—and with *Seascape,* his language and character dynamics feel wearied—his work is the result of a distinctive mind obsessively probing life's recesses for meaning."

## What Do I Read Next?

- *The Sandbox* (1959) is another play by Albee that deals with conflicts within a tense marriage.

- *Happy Days* (1961) is a play by Samuel Beckett about a couple whose relationship problems are similar to those of Nancy and Charlie.

- *Landscape* (1967) is a play by

Harold Pinter, which consists of two monologues by a couple with relationship problems. An undercurrent of the play is a desire to retreat from life.

- *All Over* (1971) is a play by Albee, which he described as a complement to *Seascape*.

- *Breaking the Watch: The Meaning of Retirement in America* (2000) is a nonfiction book that discusses aspects of retirement, including how it affects the retiree and his or her relationships.

# Sources

Albee, Edward, *Seascape: A Play,* Atheneum, 1975.

Barnes, Clive, "Albee's *Seascape* Is a Major Event," *inNew York Times,* January 27, 1975.

Beaufort, John, "New Albee Comedy on Broadway," in *Christian Science Monitor,* January 30, 1975.

Clurman, Harold, Review in the *Nation,* March 15, 1975, p. 314.

Gottfried, Martin, "Edward Albee's Latest," in *New York Post,* January 27, 1975.

Kauffmann, Stanley, Review in *The New Republic,* February 22, 1975, pp. 22, 33.

Kissel, Howard, *"Seascape,"* in *Women s Wear Daily,* January 27, 1975.

Koehler, Robert,"Albee's *Seascape* Runs Aground on Characterization," in *Los Angeles Times,* April 26, 1988.

Kroll, Jack, "Leapin' Lizards," in *Newsweek,* February 10, 1975.

Wilson, Edwin, "Disturbing Creatures from the Deep," in *Wall Street Journal,* January 28, 1975.

Winn, Steven, "A Lizard-eye View of Humanity / Wonder and Whimsy in Albee's *Seascape,*" in *San Francisco Chronicle,* October 19, 1996, p. El.

# Further Reading

Gussow, Mel, *Edward Albee: A Singular Journey,* Simon & Schuster, 1999.

> This biography covers the whole of Albee's personal and professional life and was written by a former *New York Times* theater critic.

Hirsch, Foster, *Who's Afraid of Edward Albee?,* Creative Arts Book Company, 1978.

> This monograph provides critical commentary of Albee's plays and career, from 1959 to the mid-1970s.

Kennedy, Pagan, *Platforms: A Microwaved Cultural Chronicle of the 1970s,* St. Martin's Press, 1994.

> This nonfiction book discusses social and cultural aspects of the United States in the 1970s.

Kolin, Philip C., ed., *Conversations with Edward Albee,* University of Mississippi Press, 1988.

> This is a collection of interviews with Albee, which were originally published between 1961 and 1988.

CPSIA information can be obtained
at www.ICGtesting.com
Printed in the USA
BVHW031700081122
651457BV00014B/525